One Bright Day

Poems About the Dances of Life

Barbara Welsh

ILLUSTRATED BY DONNA YANKUS

HALLARD PRESS

Cover Design, Typography & Production by Hallard Press LLC
Illustrations: Donna Yankus

Published by Hallard Press LLC.
www.HallardPress.com   Info@HallardPress.com   352-234-6099
Bulk copies of this book can be ordered at Info@HallardPress.com

Publisher's Cataloging-in-Publication data

Names: Welsh, Barbara C., author. | Yankus, Donna, illustrator.
Title: One bright day : poems about the dances of life / by Barbara C. Welsh; illustrated by Donna Yankus.
Description: The Villages, FL: Hallard Press LLC, 2022.
Identifiers: LCCN: 2022907625 | ISBN: 978-1-951188-52-8
Subjects: LCSH Poetry, American. | BISAC POETRY / American / General | POETRY / Subjects & Themes / Family | POETRY / Women Authors
Classification: LCC PS3623.E4825 O54 2022 | DDC 811.6--dc23

Printed in the United States of America   1

ISBN: 978-1-951188-52-8 (Paperback)
ISBN: 978-1-951188-58-0 (Ebook)

DEDICATION

To Michael Yankus
My cheerleader and partner in life who encourages
and inspires me on a daily basis.

Michael, Michael he's my man
If he can't do it nobody can.
He works hard throughout the day
Making my life good in every way.
He works outside to keep the landscaping looking nice and neat
Cutting grass, edging, clipping, and planting in all the heat.
He makes sure our cars and golf cart are in tip top shape
He's very organized, thoughtful and doesn't make many mistakes.
He does the grocery shopping and keeps an inventory of what we need.
He helps with dinner every night he's the perfect sous chef, he takes my lead.
We enjoy being together, have lots of fun, lend support through thick and thin.
I need to tell him everyday how much I love him and without him I'll never win.
He's the perfect man for me and the love of my life.
When I count my blessings, I'm so thankful to be his wife.

Footprints of Life / Poem on Page 13

Table of Contents

Life and Happiness

Hoping, Praying and Dancing

If we could only replace hate with love
By turning it over to our God above.
Why do we listen so much to our mainstream media
Their words certainly don't equate to an encyclopedia.

You can decide to be controlled by fear
Which won't make your worries disappear.
We're all hoping for a brand new day
When all our tears will be washed away.

If you continue to think your life is full of sorrow
You'll never look forward to a bright tomorrow.
If you can start to focus on your brand new story
Filled with hope, then you will begin to see the glory
In creating an amended and magnificent testimony.

For me, I like to dance to help take the heartache away
I can listen to music as I shuffle and sway.
Dancing fills me with a sense of grace
And I truly feel God's warm embrace.

Worry just shows the lack of faith in what happens today
But dancing allows a natural way to float away.
It erases and teaches our tendency to wonder why
And takes away the emotions that cause you to cry.

So there's a few things I do to feel more alive
And get through another day just to survive.
I turn on the music and dance away
And open my Bible and pray and pray.

In the Shadow of Love

You start to believe the whole world has gone mad
Everything you see and hear makes you so sad.
You begin to question does my life really matter
Over and over you're made to feel you must scatter.

So should we all just run and hide in a shadow of shame
Or stand up and say we too can play this game.
We are warriors and together we can remain strong
We believe in ourselves so let's prove them wrong.

We have a creator who loves and guides us and reigns from
above
Let's step out of the darkness and into His shadow of love.
God takes what is broken and makes it anew
If you open your heart His glory will shine through.

We are over-comers and protectors of our hearts
We have the power of prayer so nothing can tear us apart.
So lift your head high and feel the warmth of the sun
And always remember the battle has already been won.

Footprints of Life

Some footprints may never have a chance to be seen.
Others have been erased or lost from life's screen.
Babies lost and hearts are broken
Words are no longer spoken.
Do footprints appear in heaven
Or are we left to only question?
The footprints of regret
Never easy to let go and forget.
Footprints may be our windows to the soul
Leaving memories to be written on a scroll.
Positive or negative influences that withstand
Not just impressions we leave in the sand
Do footsteps always create footprints
Or just leave unadorned imprints?
Maybe they are one in the same
Seems so hard to explain
Footprints disappear with time
Fade away with God's design
Some never see the light of day
Others simply fade away.

The Miracle Cure

A friend is someone who makes you homemade spaghetti
    sauce
When you need support they are there with kind words and
    thoughts.
They will say a prayer asking for God's help and almighty
    grace
Which validates and restores your faith in the human race.
There is nothing better than having a good friend
Especially one who is always there and transcends
Beyond what's expected when you need a helping hand.
They cause your soul to blossom because they understand.
Be grateful if you have a friend in who you can confide
Day or night, rain or shine they will be there at your side.
A real friend is one who walks in when the rest of the world
    walks out.
If you have a problem they come running when you give them
    a shout.
A friend is strong when you're weak, brave when you're
    scared,
The magical antidote when feeling desperate and despaired.
They have a heart so full of love that it overflows to another
    person,
The remedy to overcome loneliness and the fear of desertion.
Loving, caring and selflessly giving is the miracle cure
Along with faith in God we know our futurity is assured.

The Purple Sweet Potato

I've eaten a lot of vegetables in my life
By taking a bite or using a fork and knife.
Eating them raw, boiled, steamed or microwaved
My kids had to eat more if they misbehaved.

There is always a question about the tomato
Is it a fruit or a vegetable like the potato?
Carrots, cucumbers, broccoli and peas
Can you pass me some vegetables please?

Many types of lettuce can be found
Such as Bibb, butterhead, leafy or round.
Corn, radishes, peppers and kale
If that's all we ate we'd be thin as a rail.

Beans: green, snap, French cut or sliced
Into the salad bowl chopped and or diced.
Kohlrabi, arugula, and some herbs may be hard to find
Then there is squash, never knew there are so many kinds.

I recently discovered a veggie that is purple and tastes very
    sweet
Not just because of its color but wow what a treat.
A purple sweet potato was quite a surprise plus a beautiful
    sight
It's always the little things in life that provide the most delight.

Sum of Every High and Low

A score of music consists of many notes both high and low
The steps in a dance can be choreographed to be fast or slow
A painting has hues of many colors both dark and light
Each day we have consists of morning, noon, and night
Life is composed of opposites; a sum of every high and low
Look forward to the special times that life has yet to show
Times of joy to counteract your fears and tears
It's best to focus on all the most memorable days and years
Accept the things you cannot change
Modify the actions you can rearrange
Look up, not down; keep your head held up high
Every day is a gift, be thankful you're alive.

Delicate Hearts

A heart is like a candle blowing in the wind
Fragile, delicate, but beating strong from within.
Hearts need protection and special care
To cushion and shield them from despair
Defend them from false promises and heartaches
Avoid disappointments that may lead to heartbreaks.
The heart sees and feels what is invisible to the eyes
Emotions of joy and euphoria are a few reasons why.
A difference exists between what the mind expects
And the reality of where and when love will intercept.
Affection is cultivated through the tenderness of the heart
Growing in a desire to never be apart
The heart sends a signal that this is "the one"
A new season for your delicate heart has begun.

Pandemics and Puzzles

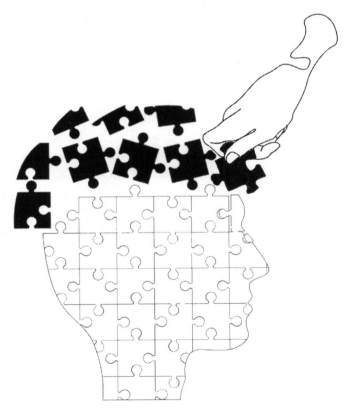

Press On

As the seasons change and your journey seems long
A heartfelt conversation with yourself will help you stay
    strong.
You need to believe you are miraculously made
In the image of greatness, no need to feel afraid.

Lift your head high and in the darkness you'll see a strong
    light
With faith you can eliminate your fear so hold on to what's
    right.
Break the chains that bind and cause you to fret
God will open his arms to comfort you so don't give up yet.

Everywhere you turn the news tries to fill you with fear
Question it, do your own research don't believe everything you
    hear.
Something has changed; what you see in the media can take
    hold
Of your mind, it may influence your thinking so you have to
    be bold.

So press on and hold on a little bit longer
And soon you will realize you feel so much stronger.
After awhile you'll be able to determine what is most true and
    honest
And what stories are false and have words and thoughts to
    abolish.

Missing Puzzle Pieces

Some people enjoy putting together a puzzle
I tried but discovered I'd rather wear a muzzle.
The intricacies and detail involved baffles my mind
Puzzle enthusiasts have patience and are one of a kind.
Beautiful scenes and pictures come to life and appear
Satisfaction is achieved when the completion is near.
Frustration sets in when a piece or two seems to be lost
Spending all this time and effort, is it worth all the cost?
The puzzler looks everywhere, did the vacuum gobble one up
Or did a piece of the puzzle fall into the morning's coffee cup.
Life is similar to a puzzle because who knows what's really in
    store
There are many missing pieces we need more time to explore.
Could one of the missing puzzle pieces in today's world be
    love?
Along with a personal relationship with our savior from up
    above.

Taking Its Toll

Snowbirds want to go home but they are stuck
Thoughts of a vacation – no such luck.
Riding in an airplane now fills you with fear
Then you must quarantine two weeks I hear.

Missing so many birthdays and school graduations
You forget what's its like to offer your congratulations.
Feeling so isolated and all alone
And no one will ever answer their phone.

In order to socialize we need to Zoom, FaceTime or Skype
Is communicating that way worth all the hype.
But how can it replace a warm embrace
And seeing our loved ones face to face.

We miss our family, friends and holiday get-togethers
Our emotions become fragile and light as feathers.
It's taking its toll and we're caught in a trap
Sometimes all you can do is just take a nap.

In the Midst of Misery

"Blinded in the midst of misery" was a statement
I heard when I turned on the TV
This type of vernacular and words were so foreign to me.
Gloom and doom was the theme that was all I could hear
I needed some way to suppress and block out the fear.

So I decided to focus on the things I can control
Obstruct all the negative so it won't take its toll.
Stop looking at social media, it can only be bad
People you used to admire now make you mad.

Here's some suggestions I learned from my friends
Concentrate on the positive and make it a trend.
First you must take a pledge to be kind
And leave the frustration you're feeling behind.

Read a book, watch a movie, sing and dance to a song
Before you know it you'll smile and it won't take that long.
Take a short hike or start riding your bike
You're bound to find something you like.

Learn a new language, plant a garden, write poetry
You may find new talents that surprise even me.
Learn to play the piano, the organ or even a guitar
Sing along, be creative you'll feel like a star.

Try a new recipe, bake a cake or a pie
Soon you will say why not, I will give it a try.
Do yard work, grow herbs, do something brand new
And you will discover there's no time to be blue.

These are some suggestions to relieve some of your sorrow
So then you can look forward to a bright new tomorrow.
The one thing I forgot that's most important of all
Thank God for your blessings you'll feel 10 feet tall.

COVID Cripples

We're afraid to go out
Shake hands, walk about
Can't travel on planes
Play cards or other games.

Too afraid to visit friends and family
Forgot my mask, oh excuse me!
Washing your hands until they look red and raw
Carrying some hand sanitizer, is that a new law?

Our favorite classes are canceled and no longer held
Dancing outside in the heat, if you feel at all compelled.
Hugs are seen as a horrible choice
Soon they won't even let us rejoice.

.
How much longer will we be asked to cope?
If you rely on the news, there is no hope.
The main theme is to promote lots of fear.
This sure is not what we want to hear.
We have become COVID cripples.
Stuck in a trap; it's really a pickle.

Looking Like What the Cat Drags In

I used to get up early, fix my hair, put on makeup and try to
    look nice
Now I look in the mirror and in horror decide if I should call
    Miami Vice.
With no reason to go out and do my normal routine
I say to myself do I look like what a cat might actually drag in?
I try to use Zoom for a special meeting or some other class
But only if I can mute myself so participants can't take a
    glance.
Is that the same lady they will murmur who danced at the
    square?
She looks like she must have had a really good scare.

That's what a quarantine can do for your self esteem.
You walk around the block just to let off some steam.
You try doing puzzles, cooking more and eating too much.
It's time to admit that this has to stop, its been long enough.
So you put on your new Mickey or Minnie Mouse mask
And decide you can venture out now you're up to the task.
Throwing all caution to the wind you go out to a store.
It wasn't so hard, you feel braver so why not try to do more.
Sometimes you have to be brave and don't live in fear.
Don't listen and fall for everything you see, read and hear.
We will all be in the nut house if this doesn't end soon
We are warriors so let's break out of this self-imposed cocoon.

Dancing and Prancing

Diddly Squats

What type of exercise should I try today?
You need several hours a week all the experts say.
Should I go for a nice walk or maybe a run
It sure doesn't sound like very much fun.
I can do some aerobics, yoga or Pilates
I need to stay motivated, how hard can it be.
Online videos, DVDs and zoom classes can also be used
Making the right decision for me just gets me confused.
Exercise is good for you there's no doubt about that
So I decided to do some of my diddly squats.

Dance Your Heartaches Away

Dance is the great equalizer
Serving as life's tranquilizer.
Dance provides a counter balance.
Remembering steps is a dancer's challenge
Patterns are formed as steps are combined.
It boosts memory as dancers soon will find.
Dance helps to relieve anxiety and stress
Improves flexibility while adding poise and grace
Helps achieve better balance and a stronger heart.
Dancing burns calories increasing energy at its start.
Beats depression attributing to a brighter mood
Creating feelings of euphoria so faith is renewed.
Pirouettes and twirls help to build confidence.
In the mind of a dancer it creates a new renaissance
Through movement and beautiful expression
Dancers convey a story, message or lesson.
They dance away hurts and heartache
So a brand new day is never far away.

This is the Dance

This is the dance
One last chance
To use all your flair
Without any care
Now is the perfect time
For you to radiate and shine
You know all the steps
You've done all the prep
Pivots, chase and spiral turns
Using all that you have learned
Cherishing and loving every moment
The perfect opportunity for atonement
Discovering the mystery of all you can be
The manifestation of beauty for all to see
Your life is one dynamic and fascinating dance
Transforming you like a whimsical romance
Maximize the effect of this innovative dance
Your once-in-a-lifetime quintessential chance
So now is the time....
And this is the place.

Barbara Welsh

The Message of Dance

Dancing soothes the soul
By easing tension and helping to console.
A dancer tells a story in a theatrical way
Using steps to form the desired display.
Choreographers create a vision.
Dancers express it with precision.
A dark or light mood may be expressed
As the movements and gestures suggest.
Dances can be dramatic to stimulate emotion
Creating a testimony of words unspoken.
Dancers find inspiration and motivation
As they become lost in the world of their creation.
Gradations of energy unfold like a rainbow after a storm.
A dynamic quality unfurls as the dancer begins to perform.
A dancer releases endorphins that trigger positive vibes
Gliding across the floor feeling more and more alive.
An art form of simple and complex movements at first glance
But picturesque and sustained beauty
Becomes the message of the dance.

Smile, Have Fun and Line Dance

Line dancing is often misunderstood.
Anyone can do it if only they would.
Just stand in a line and move your feet
Or shuffle a little until the dance is complete.
Many think line dances are only done to Country Western
songs.
Put on your cowboy boots, a hat and just dance along.
Partly true but there's much more than meets the eye.
Complicated steps and patterns must be mastered and applied.
It's not limited to the Macarena, Cupid Shuffle and Electric
Slide
Learning a new dance may take hours of practice
Before perfected and performed with some pride.
Dances are choreographed to all genres of music
Like hip hop, jazz, rock, or songs that are slow and
therapeutic.
Line dances range from beginner to advanced.
The commonality is that they can be addicting
When learned, mastered and personally enhanced.
Line dances can be simple or fairly complicated
Testing your memory each time they are duplicated.
Line dancing is popular in all parts of the world.
Why not learn a few dances and give it a whirl?
Smile, have fun, no one cares if you make a mistake.
It's not rocket science, just a line dance, there's nothing at
stake.

It's Surprising What a Dance Can Do

Feeling stressed, worries abound
Learn the newest dance that is going around.
Concentrate on the combination of steps
And suddenly your life seems less complex.
It may take some time to get it right
But with repetition it will soon take flight.
As you begin to lose yourself in the flow of patterns
Mastering each combination of steps, twists and turns
A dance turns into a hidden language of the soul.
The anxiousness you once felt loses its control.
A dance is like a dream recreated by your feet
With a theme or rhythm that follows a certain beat.
A dance becomes a timeless interpretation of life
Music comes alive to help relieve the initial strife.
A dance creates and amplifies a joyful mood for you
When in doubt, dance it out...
It's surprising what a dance can do!

The Power of Dance

Dance is a powerful form of human expression
An antidote for a negative outlook and mild depression.
Dance is a way to communicate through movement
Providing a pattern for recreation and amusement.
While conveying the whole range of human emotions
A dancer tells a story like a highly disciplined theologian.
Dancing strengthens, disciplines and refreshes the soul
Whether watching or participating, entertainment is its goal.
When someone is dancing they feel enlightened and inspired
Through a compelling performance that may have transpired.
Dancers use it to celebrate, mourn, communicate and express.
Once your feet start moving the elation is hard to repress.
The music, rhythm, steps and choreography all play a part
However, dancing is magical when you dance with your heart.

The Balance Beam

Walking on a balance beam
Not as easy as it might seem
One foot in front of the other like a needle and thread
Looking neither left or right but always straight ahead.
Did you ever go hiking expecting to walk on mostly solid
    ground?
Recently this wasn't the case and not what a group of hikers
    found.
The path required waking on planks to avoid deep water from
    all the rain.
It was unexpected and uneven, good balance was needed to
    follow the grain
Of wooden boards set up to avoid having to go through deep
    water and mud.
Balance was crucial to avoid tumbling, creating a domino
    effect and a big thud.
Our hiking group faced this dilemma just the other day.
Staying on course was the key and concentration was in play.
On a balance beam in the woods or in life you will see
A perfect connection of mind, body and soul is what needs to
    be.
Everything in moderation; avoid excesses or extremes if you
    can.
Living with faith and harmony in your life is a good balancing
    plan.

Inside Out

Turned Inside Out

The world seems inside out.
There is wrong and there is right.
The difference was once in plain sight.
Things seem to have changed
They have been rearranged
What we thought we believed
Becomes mixed up and tossed around with confusion
So doubt and uncertainty has now been achieved.

In the eyes of the minority, we seem wrong
Long-standing values need to remain strong.
What happened to the concept of rugged individualism
Have we succumbed to the abandonment of any realism?
What's changed? Is it our right to remain self reliant
To stop capitulating and be forced to act so compliant.

Political correctness has taken a turn for the worst
We are afraid that what we say could be widely dispersed.
Our words are taken the wrong way we often fear
Even though we ourselves see them as very clear.

It's upside down and turned all around.
Through hope and determination we can't go wrong.
With faith in Almighty God who provides us a solid base
That no one can ever truly erase.
Get on your knees and pray for Him to come into your life
To achieve personal peace that transcends beyond all belief
And helps to provide a divine form of solid relief.

Less Stress, More Yes

Are you disappointed, don't think you have what it takes?
Start believing in yourself; stand strong to finish this race.
Slow down, your thoughts may be revolving at too fast a pace.
Listen for what's true to help understand and make sense of it
    all.
Don't concentrate on your problems, it will only cause you to
    fall.
Start a new plan that focuses on more fulfillment and joy.
Build a bedrock of prayer and faith for a meaningful life to
    enjoy.
Days are passing by too quickly; you need to limit anxiety and
    stress.
A permanent anchor is needed that remains strong and
    steadfast.
Turn to God as your anchor and take the focus off of yourself
The fear and uncertainty you're feeling will fall off from the
    shelf.

Sand Traps and Hiccups

Would it be a perfect world
If there were no sand traps or hiccups?
In golf, sand traps are places to avoid
In order to maintain a low score.
Hiccups are like sand traps
They come out of nowhere
How can this be really fair?
A good case of hiccups
Can be embarrassing for sure
It's not easy to find a cure.
Is it unrealistic to expect smooth sailing
Throughout your life without ever failing?
Facing challenges and difficulties
Definitely can lead to strife
There's no such thing as a perfect life.
Give thanks to God for all your blessings
Including those sand traps and hiccups
They define you, making you unique
Molding you with life's identifying etchings.

Tip of the Tongue

Have you ever tried to remember
The name of a person, a movie or a song that was sung
But your mind is blank, it just sits on the tip of your tongue.
You try naming every letter in the alphabet going from A to Z
But no matter how hard you try it just won't break free.

So you get all worked up
And say my memory's all shot
Or my brain's in a knot
So you cheat and give Alexa a shot.

Although it doesn't seem so logical
There is a designated name for this phenomena
The tip of the tongue syndrome
Not very well known; its called Lethologica.

Defined in the dictionary as an inability to remember
A particular word or name so you may think you're on a
    bender.
It's sometimes classified as a lifestyle disease
Kin to when you look all over and can't find your keys.

Or when your phone is not found with ease
So all you can say is geez.
Or you'll search for your glasses and swear they have fled
And then you'll discover they're on top of your head.

Please don't be discouraged it happens to the best of us
So it's not really worth making a big fuss
Or thinking it may only get any worse.
Have a glass of wine or a drink of your choice
I'm sure you'll feel much better in due course.

A Bad Day for a Bank Robbery

When is it a bad day for a bank robbery?
When you go to a cashless bank
Or when you get there your mind goes blank
When someone is at the end of their rope
And there seems to be little or no hope.
Is that a good day to plan a robbery
Especially when there's the threat of personal poverty?
It invariably seems like everyone has a perfect life
Their daily posts show they are prosperous and free from strife
Videos and photos document a life of perfection
Sadly your life seems to be going in a different direction.
Is anyone really satisfied today
Do too many choices get in the way?
Constantly presented with endless alternatives
Decisions must always be superlative.
Many things you may have thought of as wrong
Now are accepted as okay and seem to belong.
Maybe today is a perfect day to rob a bank
Only if you convince the police it's merely a prank.

Needless Worries

Left to themselves needless worries and cares
Can lead to feelings of despondency and despair.
In their midst, turn over to God the troubles in your life
To guide you through tumultuous situations and strife.
In troublesome times, He provides protection and hope
That fear will not become a slippery slope
That catapults into a loss of faith and purpose.
Visualize the calmness of a glistening freshwater surface.
Resolve needles worries by establishing loyalty and trust.
Develop harmony by learning how to readjust.
God's compassion is like a warm blanket of comfort
Assuring that your peace of mind will be triumphant.

Tickling Your Funny Bone

The Cockroach Encounter

Last night in our bathroom I ran into a cockroach
He scattered away as I tried to approach.
He suddenly reappeared and acted quite pensive
He sat there without moving and was not very offensive.

I had heard these insects are common and hardy
But usually depicted as big, black and dirty.
Read once they have existed for a very long time as you would
    agree
At least 320 million years, can be quite social, oh no I think he
    sees me.

Since I was still sleepy and he was doing me no harm
I crawled back in my bed and slept like a charm.
The next day I awoke and wondered if it was all just a dream
Then realized it wasn't when my wife started to scream.

The Perpetual Teenager

We like to think we can do all the things we did when we were
  a teen.
Bike and hike for ten to twenty miles a day or something in
  between.
Dance all day and swing and sway way into the night
Spin around in circles and allemande left and right.
Drink one too many cocktails expecting not to feel a thing
Until the next morning when your head pulses and packs a big
  fat sting.
Zumba, yoga, Pilates, and ballet classes all done on the same
  day
Then go out at night, enjoy some music and dance the night
  away.
It's all okay until one day when you start feeling some aches
  and pains.
So if your birthday is coming up and you don't want to face
  the truth.
I'll share a simple **makeup** tip that helps me feel like I'm still
  in my youth.
Just **make up** an age you wish to be and always stick to your
  story
Then you will remain a perpetual teenager with all its
  youthful glory.

Laughing, Smiling, and Silly Jokes

You've heard the saying "laughter is the best medicine."
One person laughs then another and all are forced to grin.
There is nothing in the world so irresistibly contagious
As laughter, good humor and a smile; it's so advantageous.
It cures a multitude of ills and is wine for the soul.
Sometimes it's good to feel giggly and out of control.
A good hearty laugh will relieve physical tension and stress.
It gives your immune system a boost so why not give it a test.
Don't allow anxiety and depression to take control.
Give yourself permission to just let go.
Take time to relax, don't allow fear to take hold so you buckle.
It is definitely time to have an uncontrollable chuckle.
Learn a few silly jokes and tell them to friends with a slight
      sigh
To determine if they will laugh or cry.
Let me give it a try.......
I can only remember 25 letters of the alphabet and I don't
      know Y.
Why did the chicken go to the park? To get to the other slide.
I told my girlfriend she had drawn her eyebrows on too high.
She looked surprised.
I hope this little poem made you smile.
At least for just a little while.
It's an unprecedented time for us all.
So have faith, rise up, and stand tall.

Missing Slipper versus a Missing Sock

Is it worse to lose a slipper or a sock?
I think to lose a slipper is much worse.
Because it is much harder to try to replace.
A sock can be added to another similar pair
To provide an extra in case one gets a hole or a tear.
Also you can't blame the dryer or the washer's design
For losing a sock you searched everywhere not to find.
Maybe the sock is stuck to your underwear due to static cling.
With a slipper that can't be an excuse or really a thing.
Maybe you have never faced exactly this same dilemma
You're more organized and it hasn't caused a problem.
I work hard everyday not to lose something so vital as my
    mind
Unlike a sock or a slipper it's irreplaceable because it's an
    original design.

A Seasick Crocodile

Have you ever seen a seasick crocodile?
The vision can pile up lots of bile and vile.
We used to say see ya later alligator
And follow it up with after awhile crocodile.
Okay let's get back to the original question at hand
To solve this puzzle and take somewhat of a stand.
Does a crocodile ever really get seasick?
And make a mad dash to hide away lickety-split.
Then take a dose of his motion sickness medicine, Crock-a-
    Meen
So embarrassed and upset he would rather not be seen.
Ruining his reputation and no longer viewed as ferocious and
    wild
Scared that he will now be known as only timid and mild.
If crocodiles get sea sick do they always go somewhere to
    hide?
Or try to camouflage themselves by turning over on one side.
Maybe this is all a fake rumor and just a big crock
He may just like to have fun; sing and dance to the crocodile
    rock.
Maybe he ate too many bugs or choked on someone's long-lost
    sock.
Thinking about it may cause laughter if you picture it for very
    long.
Somebody may even use this situation to compose a poem or a
    song.
Don't lose any sleep over it, your mind might start to implode
That might be better than seeing a seasick crocodile start to
    unload.

The Hand of God

Power Lights

There is a light inside of everyone that tells a story.
The brighter it shines the more it shows each brilliant glory.
Brokenness will be dimmed and then snuffed out for good.
Power lights to help visualize a love and faith often
    misunderstood.
Each personal light glows radiantly because it is yours alone
A reflection of Christ within that grows stronger whenever
    shone.
So powerful that it forgives and conquers the darkness of sin.
And reveals the most powerful light of Christ that lies within.
Projecting and radiating so it can't be hidden from all to see
Developing a meaningful purpose that benefits both you and
    me
So productive it establishes a need for salvation to end the
    darkness
Shining the bright light of hope that honors our Lord's holy
    goodness.
The light is forever turned on and the electric bill has been
    fully paid.
The groundwork for eternal life has been carefully and
    divinely laid.

In Your Silent Night

Hold back tears
So no one hears
Love will come and find you
Your heart believes it's true
Fears and worries hide from sight
In the silence that fills the night
Where heaven hears your song
And distant singers hum along
Silhouettes of dancers pass by
Causing you to question why
Broken hearts do not always mend
When daylight fades and comes to an end
As night begins and darkness arrives
Hope and aspirations come alive
Now you know that you will survive
Faith is restored
A prayer is heard
In your silent night.

Without You

Without You, life has no meaning
Feeling unsettled and backwards leaning
Like rain when you're on the beach
You have no control, it is out of reach.
How can people be so blind?
They often seem so unkind.
Something is missing in their life.
Words they speak cut like a knife.
You do not know what they're going through
Don't judge or think what may not be true.
Instead offer them a lifeline so they can connect
To a refuge that provides a shield to protect.
Let them know that He is waiting for them.
He patiently watches and does not condemn.
He loves them from the very start
Until they truly believe in their heart
That everything worthy in life is spiritually true
Because it starts and ends with You.

My Rock, My Hope

Sometimes I feel lost and agitated
Until hope that is divine fills my heart
And becomes supersaturated
With love and humility I focus on the truth.
Steadiness and stability is what I choose
Lifting me higher in my lowest valley.
A reason for my existence is kept alive
By lifting me high so I can survive.
You're my earthly anchor and solid rock
Serving hourly as my sacred daily clock
Keeping me safe when I am weary
Surrounded by your love so I'm no longer teary
Sending joy when my heart is heavy
Nothing can stand against me now
Hurt and pain blocked and not allowed
Mountains may fall into the sea
But my rock, my hope looks out for me
Cleansing me from my sins to purify
So I will praise, worship and glorify
Your sacred and most holy name
Forever changed and not the same.

A Gentle Whisper in the Noise

You are forever by my side.
A constant comfort you do provide.
An anchor to hold me steady in time of trouble.
Providing strength to handle struggle.
An ultimate display of love is there for me
Along with faith so I believe what I cannot see.
I hear your gentle voice in all the noise
To subdue anxiety and turn worry into joy.
When I think I am not strong
You tell me softly that I am wrong.
When words of doom and gloom is all I hear.
You give me hope to calm my fear.
Even though I have to walk through some darkness.
I will control and conquer evil with your mighty harness.
This gentle whisper tells me not to be afraid.
Because I am wonderfully and skillfully made.

Into the Darkness You Shine

Helplessness abounds
Division surrounds
So much confusion and deceit
Not trusting, feeling defeat
Fears enhance concerns
Uncertainty now returns
Our future is at stake
What difference can we make?

But into the darkness You shine
Awesome in power by design
Always amazing us with Your mercy
Even though we may feel unworthy
A mighty healer You always will be
Giving hope that we long to see
Trusting that You are in control
So healing can start to take a role
Moving us forward out of the darkness
Into a new light to conquer loneliness.

Barbara Welsh

By Your Side

He's by your side whenever you're falling
Answering prayers whenever you're calling
His hands are holding you
Never wavering, always true.
Although your heart may be broken
You know you'll never be forsaken.
Even in the dead of night
You're never out of His sight.
No need to carry a burden on your own
You will never have to face it all alone.
Worry and fear will disappear
And hope becomes your new veneer.
There is no reason to be afraid
You have been perfectly remade
Redeemed and restored
By your side forevermore.

Happy Holidays

Frightful or Delightful

Halloween can be frightful or delightful.
Which do you want to be?
What do you prefer to see?

Goblins, ghosts, witches and monsters are frightful.
Princesses, beauty queens, and ballerinas are delightful.
Black cats, devils, werewolves, gangsters and skeletons are
    eerie.
Mermaids, brides, fairies, movie stars, and flamingos are
    cheery.

Halloween comes around on October 31st each year.
As fall begins, children know the day is getting near.
Jack-o-lanterns are lit, young masqueraders fill the streets
Trick-or-treaters go door to door to collect yummy treats.

Originated from ancient Celtic harvest festivals and pageants
    we are told.
Now parades and costume parties provide fun for the young
    and old.
Halloween can be dark and spooky and often very scary
Or it's bright and blissful so everyone feels quite merry.

American Thanksgiving Traditions

Thanksgiving began in 1863 and now is an annual American
    tradition
Celebrated on the 4th Thursday in November without
    opposition.
Family and friends look forward to gathering for a home-
    cooked meal
A time in the Fall to celebrate and cherish each other with
    great zeal.

Thanksgiving is a day to give thanks for the blessings of life
Memories of a simpler time when there was little or no strife.
Family traditions, favorite foods, good things to eat
All come together to make Thanksgiving Day complete.

The day begins by watching the Macy's Thanksgiving Day Parade
As a traditional Thanksgiving meal is being skillfully made.
The menu features turkey, stuffing, cranberry sauce and
    pumpkin pie.
As the blessing is offered, an awareness of thankfulness
    cannot be denied.

Everyone at the table shares what they are most thankful for
While others watch football and shout for their team to score.
Other traditions include the breaking of the wishbone
Along with contacting family members who may be home
    alone.

Let us not forget the freedom we have to congregate together
To live life abundantly with all the conveniences we treasure.
We ask God to change one-sided outlooks and selfish attitudes
And to unite Americans as they offer praise and sincere
    gratitude.

Christmas Snow Globes

At Christmas time snow globes are frequently seen all around
Enclosing a miniaturized winter scene with snow falling down.
Snowmen, reindeer, Santa Claus, mistletoe or holly may appear
To show that Christmas is coming soon or is very near.
If there was a snow globe that depicts a happy scene from your
    life
A memory of a Christmas past, a day of joy without any strife
What would you choose
If there is nothing for you to lose?
Would it be a Christmas morning when you were a child
Waiting for Santa with anticipation that was hard to hide?
Perhaps a happy memory when you were first in love
Standing under mistletoe like a star-struck turtle dove?
Or a scene commemorating your baby's first Christmas morn
A delightful time when you lived each day for that little
    newborn?
This year many people are distraught because they feel so
    alone.
Their only contact with loved ones is by video or talking on
    the phone.
So try to picture a snow globe showcasing the newborn baby
    Jesus
Demonstrating God's love in a snow globe so we see the real
    reason
To promote healing and renewed strength throughout this
    season
His birth brought great joy into the world, a snow globe for all
    time.
The son of God arrives on earth providing hope and peace
    sublime.

Be My Valentine

Will you be my valentine is a question asked once a year
Both friends and lovers, young and old wait anxiously to hear.
Love, romance and good feelings are in the air.
Flowers, candy, and greeting cards are exchanged
Special celebrations and dinner dates arranged
What if every day was Valentine's Day?
When simple acts of kindness are displayed in many ways.
Sympathy is exhibited for those we may not fully understand
Generosity and helpfulness come naturally to lend a helping
     hand.
Listening intently to someone and showing your concern
A path to understanding and compassion is what you will
     learn.
Helen Keller once said "love is like a beautiful flower."
Its fragrance lingers in your memory like a soft afternoon
     shower.
When another person's happiness is more important than your
     own
Making Valentine's Day a daily observance so harmony is fully
     known.

St. Patrick's Day

Parades, festivals, singing Danny Boy and wearing green
Are a few things that St. Patrick's Day may mean
Bag pipes playing, marching bands and fire brigades
Along with leprechauns and shamrocks on display
Corned beef and cabbage is a traditional Irish dish
If you're Irish, you may be lucky so make a wish
March 17th is the traditional day to celebrate
The feast of St Patrick is what the Irish commemorate.
It is actually the day that St Patrick died.
It was a time when the Irish people cried.
Christianity was introduced to Ireland at this time
Another reason to give thanks, say a prayer
And listen for the cathedral bells to chime.
I recall the Irish brogue that my Great Grandmother had
I think of her warm and kind smile and it makes me glad
That I can still remember her with love on St Patrick's day
So I give tribute to her in a fond and tenderhearted way.

The Easter Bunny, the Jewel, and the Prize

The Easter Bunny is a folkloric figure
Hopping here and there with joyful vigor.
Bringing colored eggs, candy, and sometimes toys
In his basket for well-behaved girls and boys.
Easter is known for Easter egg hunts and family fun
When flowers bloom in the warmth of the sun.
Easter is a joyous holiday marked by a time of renewal
When we rejoice and give thanks for our eternal Jewel.
Easter confirms our belief that God's love never dies
We are forgiven, Christ has risen, the true Easter Prize.

May is the Month for Mothers

Mothers are gentle, mothers are kind
Sometimes they have to be strict and spank your behind.
I know that my mom loved me it was easy to tell
But when I didn't follow the rules she sure gave me hell.
Discipline is necessary as I later learned when I had kids of
my own.
Being consistent is hard but in the long run the benefits are
shown.
My mother gave me support through good times and bad.
She always had a caring shoulder to cry on whenever I was
sad.
A mother is always ready to give comfort and provide
nurturing care
With a tender heart and warm embrace she willingly shares.
She teaches how to know the difference between right and
wrong
Encouraging you to be successful by remaining steady and
strong.
As you grow older you learn to appreciate your mother even
more
You realize that she is part of your being right down to the
core.
When you lose your mother, a part of you dies
Memories and keepsakes bring tears to your eyes.
Mother's Day is a time to give tribute and honor to your
mother
A chance to give thanks for her, you only get one, there is no
other.

Memorial Day

Memorial Day is a holiday also known as Decoration Day
Celebrated every year on the last Monday in May.
It is a day to honor American military personnel
Who have sacrificed their lives in wars they fought.
We should never forget what it was they sought.
They died for our freedom, the right as a country to exist.
It's an annual holiday to show our respect and not to dismiss.
Therefore be thankful that you live in a country like no other.
Learn from the past and you will discover
You can be a force for positive change
Not criticize our history and try to rearrange.
God will continue to bless this country
Protect us from enemies and keep us free
As we praise Him from sea to shining sea.

Happy Birthday America

July 4th, 1776 is a special birthday that we celebrate each year
The birth of our nation that deserves jubilation and cheer.
The Declaration of Independence paved the way for the
    American dream.
It affirms that all people are created equal and held with
    esteem.
Our founding fathers took many risks to provide these gifts
Of freedom, the pursuit of happiness and justice for all.
With a promise to not settle for less, they answered the call.
Today is a day to honor our founders and the sacrifices they
    made
With hope that the values of integrity and truth would never
    fade.
They established a new nation to offer these inalienable rights.
To make certain God always will keep us in His sight.
Pray that our hearts will turn toward God
To ensure that He continues to pour out His blessing
Protecting our right to live free and avoid regressing.
The Pledge of Allegiance should remain unchanged
And The Bill of Rights and our Constitution not rearranged.
We must accept our differences and be thankful we live in the
    USA.
Victory will come for those who walk in faith and continue to
    pray
With confidence that our country as founded will never be led
    astray.

Christmas Sparkle

Is it the lights on your Christmas tree
That create the sparkle you feel and see
Or the jingling bells you hear on Christmas night
And the glistening of a star shining so bright?
Could it be the holiday spirit you feel in the air
And the giving of gifts that show you care?
Is it the sparkle you notice in your grandchildren's eyes
Waiting for Santa to arrive with gifts and new surprises?
Although heartwarming moments reflect the joy of the season,
Does the birth of Jesus resonate as the actual reason?
Because our savior is a permanent gift from God to you
And so many presents are forgotten in a month or two.
There's more to Christmas than often meets the eye
As the Christmas star shines and sparkles in the dark sky.
It appeared in the nativity story as a sign of God's love
To direct the wisemen as it shown from high above.
The sparkling star guided them to their destination
A miraculous sign fulfilling a prophecy of determination.
Hidden in the light and sparkle is the truth
You can learn to accept it in faith if you choose
A truth to bring healing and peace to all mankind
When the genuine Christmas sparkle is what you find.

Just Another Day or a New Beginning

The first day of a new year
Can surely bring some fear
Is it just another day?
Or the beginning of a different way?
Having the courage to start over
Like a literary or musical composer
Stepping out of your comfort zone
But not wanting to do it all alone
Getting a glimpse of fresh possibilities
Someone to help add a touch of positivity
Along with a pinch of determination
Searching for a new purpose and direction
Asking God for forgiveness and protection
It is what you decide you want your life to be
Fixing your eyes on a future you would like to see
A daily blueprint of love and hope to fill your heart
Along with a beautiful ray of sunshine to jump start.

Your Place in this World

Barbara Welsh

Everyone Has a Story to Tell

Footprints on the sands of time
Like a bell getting ready to chime
A walking heartache may be what's at hand
Time to release the pain and take a stand.
Your story can be a testimony that needs to be heard
Relatable situations that have occurred
Can make a lasting effect and begin a trend
To help a broken heart to heal and mend
Are you too wrapped up in your own personal worry?
That you lack understanding for someone else's story.
A sympathetic ear and a heart that's warm
Can lend comfort and start to quell the storm
Redemption cleanses and makes us well
When everyone has a story to tell.

Looking for a Breakthrough

Anne Murray once sang…
"We sure could use a little good news…"
Listening to these lyrics today may cause the blues.
It seems like bad news is all around
And there is little hope to be found.
The world seems inside out
Our minds are filled with doubt.
Longing to have a voice
Seems like a simple choice.
Take what's broken; finding a way to mend
Reaching out for healing and a message to send
Believing there will be a breakthrough
A defender of hearts to pursue
Trusting that change is on the horizon
Opening a path for rays of sunshine
Shades of doubt will fade away
Expecting that better news is on its way
A breakthrough of fairness, peace and comfort
Knowing in the end God will be triumphant
Good news is just around the corner
God has the resolution for all disorder.

Pot Stirrers

Dennis the Menace often *stirs the pot*
Gets in trouble on the spot
Quick to agitate a situation
Without a plausible explanation
Mischief is his middle name
Always has someone else to blame
Pot stirrers, like Dennis the Menace, are all around
Wherever they go drama abounds
Like a bull in a china shop
Causing trouble is their plot
Some people enjoy stirring the pot
Gossiping and always pushing the limits
Getting more fired up with every minute
Always a troublemaker like a pebble in your shoe
Becomes a thorn in your side through and through
Shaking things up and adding some spice
May be funny to some
But to others naughty, not nice.

The Best Me

I'm the best me when I'm with you.
Forever in my heart, I always knew
I am best when I know I don't have to be perfect
Confident enough to commit to love and receive respect.

Constantly caring, always there
A closeness shared that seems so rare
Understanding how and when to show affection
Because of a strong, secure and solid connection.

Forgiving, accepting the past, loving the present
Having fun, laughing, glowing and luminescent
Going through life together, sticking like glue
Cannot imagine life without you.

Letting go of past mistakes and regret
Making memories impossible to forget
Like the moon shining in the middle of a dark night
Together we create a prismatic sparkle forever bright.

Finding Your Purpose

Everyone has a purpose
Looking for a way to surface
Aligning with God's will
Designed for you to fulfill.
Your purpose should line up with God's plan.
Before you were born this unique design began
Determining what your divine purpose was going to be.
You may not like or expect it or initially agree.
Doing your own thing may not always coincide.
Letting God be your leader and personal guide
Takes the guess work out of having to decide
As you start to progress with a sense of pride.
There may be some growing pains involved
Imperfection is not always easily resolved.
Compromise should not be a part of the package.
Clearing out or dropping some of the baggage
May be necessary to clarify God's intention for you
Before joy and personal fulfillment can break through.
Be inspired each day when you find and follow His plan;
A heavenly blueprint on which your heart and soul can stand.

Making the World a Better Place

If you think before you speak
You may not feel so bleak
When you wish you could take it back
Or beat around the bush getting way off track.
Ask yourself if what you're about to say
Will help to improve someone's day
And make the world a better place
By providing encouragement in every case.
Are your words positive, uplifting, and useful
Or unnecessary, exaggerated and untruthful?
How well do you listen before you speak?
Speaking less and listening more is a worthwhile technique.
Listen carefully to God who will always tell you what to say
You'll be surprised by the wise sentiments that you convey.
Many times God may instruct you to say nothing at all.
Staying silent is a sagacious act that often does enthrall.
We have the power to make the world a better place
If we speak as a witness to God's almighty grace.

A Ray of Sunshine in a Dark Sky

Sometimes a smile can be a ray of sunshine in a dark sky
When you're stuck in a gloomy place and don't know why.
One friendly face has the power to brighten your day
And should never be underestimated in any way.
A smile expresses compassion when shared;
It sends a message that someone sincerely cares.
A simple act of kindness and a friendly gesture
Can be like a warm blanket with a luxurious texture.
Smiling is contagious and fends off anxiety and stress.
It spins a powerful web of joy and happiness;
Causing a chain reaction that further illuminates.
A sincere smile launches optimism that percolates.
A simple grin can activate an unrestrained effusion
Splendor coming from the sky that's not an illusion.
When traveling through deep waters God is always with you
As the sun rises shining on a new day so life starts anew.

A Little Advice

A Box of Tissues

Do you ever feel like a full box of tissues?
Unable to deal with all of today's issues
Never expressing your true feelings
Or wanting to have any personal dealings.
Inside you feel really sad.
Afraid that you'll make someone mad
Keeping everything inside to avoid getting hurt
Getting so frustrated that the anger may cause an alert
It becomes impossible to stuff anymore in
And never a good strategy in which you will win
Until one day the excess anxiety starts to pop out
You need to release the fear and all of that doubt.
Don't let it get to a point of no return.
There are so many ways to relax and re-learn
How to feel perfectly safe, happy and content
Lessen the stress and begin a new plan of intent
So you never feel like your mind could implode
Or like a stuffed box of tissues that needs to explode.
Clear out the negative and focus on the positive
Let go and let God be your life's first prerogative.

Shoulditis

Have you ever heard of the condition called Shoulditis?
It's different from tendinitis, bursitis or arthritis.
Many of its symptoms you may never have considered
Look closely, take inventory and don't get bewildered.

Do you think you **should** please others before you please
    yourself?
You don't want to offend other people so you put your true
    feelings up on a shelf
Should you always be the giver and feel guilty receiving from
    others.
If you let someone give you comfort you feel guilty and
    smothered.

You believe you **should** never lose your cool
And not give in to emotional extremes as a rule.
You think you **should** always say yes to someone's request
Then get mad at yourself because you really wanted to rest.

It may not be easy to make changes but very worthwhile
Try dropping a few of these *shoulds* and start to re-file.
We all suffer from shoulditis in some degree
Never fatal, it's controllable I think you'll agree.

Ask God for his guidance to ensure that you remain in control
He loves and protects you so Shoulditis will not not take its
    toll.

In a Pickle

There are many kinds of pickles that we can choose to eat
Dill, kosher, bread & butter, gherkins, sour, and sweet.
But have you ever been in a pickle?
Or accused of being a little fickle?
How did this phrase come about, I'm in a pickle?
Literally, being in a pickle might really tickle.
It's a predicament to be stuck in the middle without a voice
In trouble like sitting on a powder keg without another choice.
Do you suddenly find yourself in a difficult situation or
  quandary?
You can't decide whether to go to a party or do the laundry.
In a pickle is a 16th century Dutch phrase: *in de pekel*
Meaning someone is quite drunk; the actual translation
Forced to call Uber for their next form of transportation
Disoriented, mixed up and feeling confused.
What a pretty pickle? You feel like you're being used.
Have you ever gone shopping and lost your car?
You can't find where you parked, it can't be too far.
You walk up and down aisles using your remote.
No car beeps back, you're in a pickle, just like the quote.
Then you remember, it was the golf cart you did drive.
Yippee, you stepped out of your pickle and still are alive.

Pat on the Back

A *job well done* are words everyone likes to hear.
Encouragement and praise resonates very clear.
Being appreciated is like a pat on the back
Creates a desire to keep going to keep on track.
Like music to the soul and a spark of hope
Providing confidence to widen the scope
The world would be a happier place
If we stopped acting like we're in a race.
A simple act of kindness goes a long way
Like offering a sincere complement every day.
What you give out comes back to you
Respecting others will make it easy to do
When positivity trumps negativity and doom and gloom
Cheerful and happy feelings will start to bloom.

Overthinking

Don't overthink every decision and action you make
Clear the slate, go relax, try baking a cake
Be happy, be positive and just let things flow
Don't think you have to be always on the go
Overthinking is a twisted form of personal fear
Worry and negative thoughts are all that you hear.
When you think about something too much or for too long
A self-imposed magnifying glass makes it look very wrong.
Overthinking leads to problems that don't exist in the first
    place
Immediately jumping to the worst conclusion in most every
    case.
Believe it or not, you can break your own heart
Ruin the situation and tear yourself all apart.
Become unproductive and keep spinning your wheels
Losing control; not knowing how you should feel.
Try stepping away from this maniacal track
Start cutting yourself a little more slack
Begin believing that all things are possible
Then you can become truly unstoppable
Optimism will take over and overthinking will fade
You'll soon feel like you have it *made in the shade!*

Clear Choices

Facts and truths are part of being both honest and humble.
Staying silent sometimes is the best way not to stumble.
Thinking before blurting something out saves you anguish
    later.
Wisdom prevails over remarks that do not make a situation
    greater.
Drama and theatrics used to get a point across reflect
    insecurity.
Using restraint and speaking from the heart demonstrates
    maturity.
Focus on what really matters and care enough to tell the truth.
Distorting what's real eventually will backfire and further
    confuse.
The only clear choice is to lean on God and not the ways of
    the world.
It then becomes God's choice to allow His blessings to be
    unfurled.
Don't sit on the bench or procrastinate; choose to lead the way.
Emerge as a powerful shining light of faith and stability on
    display.
We live in a world where dishonesty and hypocrisy are
    mainstream
Greed, lust and entitlement are no longer the extreme.
We have an option to turn away from the negative forces
By allowing God to steer us towards clear and unobstructed
    choices.

How to Put Your Foot Down for Dummies

I told my friend to stop acting like a flamingo
So finally she had to put her foot down!

Sometimes you just have to put your foot down.
An important idiom that is heard all around town.
Here are a few things to know to help you stay strong:
Avoid being indecisive so things don't go wrong.
Always adopt a firm policy when faced with opposition.
Use your authority to avoid a compromising position.
Tell someone to stop doing something in which you disagree.
This will shut down an unfortunate situation that's not meant
    to be.
Put your foot down about something you really don't want to
    do.
The more bunk you put up with, the more bunk that comes to
    you.
Stand up for yourself, it doesn't mean you have to be unkind.
Never feel bad for being assertive and speaking your mind.
Become very clear about your intentions and desires.
Agreeing to disagree is often what is required.
The doors will open up for you as a result.
You can put your foot down and still be an adult.
God gave you a purpose, you're alive for a reason.
This is your time to shine, this is your season.

Caution and Restraint

Before you post your opinion on social media
And these ideas resonate as schizophrenia
It is wise to practice caution and restraint
Or be bombarded with numerous complaints.
Anything personal, political or controversial
Once out there is henceforth not reversible.
It might make you feel better temporarily
But readers may disagree and think contrarily.
Recipients could be a friend, family member or professor
Causing resentment that may metastasize or start to fester.
Distant feelings can result and remain for quite awhile
Better not to respond or risk turning it increasingly hostile.
Open discussion and debate is a fairer substitution.
Simply letting it go is plausibly the healthiest solution.
Because the smartest and wisest person in the virtual room
Is the one who remains silent; a lesson you'll learn very soon.

Barbara Welsh

Packing a Suitcase

Getting packed to go on a trip:
What clothes should I pick?
Will it be hot or cold?
Should I bring new clothes or old?
Do I need a sweater or a hat?
A little of this, a little of that?
If it rains, I'll need an umbrella.
What if I contract salmonella?
I checked my packing list
What have I missed?
Do I have a good book?
How will those shoes look?
Did I pack my toothbrush?
I'm trying not to rush.
Settle down, don't fret
No need to be upset
Once you arrive
You'll be glad you're alive.
When your grandkids
Give you a big hug and a kiss
You'll realize all you did miss
During these past years.
So here come the tears
It was worth all the fuss
No more to discuss!

One Bright Day

Barbara Welsh

One Bright Day

One day anger and resentment will no longer be seen in our
    eyes
Replaced with peace and happiness, it shouldn't be a surprise
Now the truth will be known and cannot hide in disguise.

Fear will no longer be able to find a sustainable place.
Faith will move in to take over; fear forever erased.
The enemy will be forced to leave
So that healing can finally be achieved.

Brokenness will all be gone
Happiness will come along.

It's up to you to be first to shine forth your sparkling new light
A strong reflection of goodness and mercy that will be ever so
    bright.
It will radiate all around us and can't be contained
God's light will shine through us and not be estranged.

Our own little light can shine through a song we sing
Or a thoughtful small gift we decide to bring
A dance we perform will express our delight
An instrument of music played in the night.

There will be no denying that there's a fire in our soul
A flame that burns brightly and continues to grow.
We will know that Jesus is the reason for healing our land
He will forgive us of our sins if we just take his hand.
One bright day is not as far away as it may seem
It will be here if we pray and not think it's only a dream.

New Song, New Dance, New Chance

You found me in a desperate place
And no matter what I did face
I was rescued by your almighty grace.

Because I met you
I'm no longer blue
I found something so true
I was born again and made new.

All is made right that before seemed wrong
And now I will sing a brand new song
It's a lovely song of hope
Now I am better able to cope.

I have learned to let things go
And take it much more slow.
My debt is gone
I can move along
With a better chance
To begin my new dance.

The steps are very easy to follow
Now I have a tremendous joy
To fill in what once was hollow.
Your overwhelming love
Has lifted me high above.

So I will sing a new song
Dance a new dance
Receive a new chance
All because I met you.

Burning Bridges

Burning bridges will destroy the path you're on.
So an alternative course can no longer be found.
A little advice when responding on social media.
Try not to sound like you are an encyclopedia.
There are some things that are better left unsaid.
Try keeping your emotions in check instead.
Whether it's Facebook, Twitter, Instagram, or email
Don't offend and be known for leaving a negative trail.
Friendships and/or relationships can be destroyed.
Good judgement and restraint should be employed.
Better to have an open and honest conversation
Express your feelings openly to avoid a bad situation.
Realize how foolish it is to burn your bridges.
Be careful not to create some permanent ridges.
It might feel great in the heat of the moment.
Only to be sorry for acting like a hostile opponent.
Don't say things when you are upset.
You'll wish you hadn't and feel regret.
Kenny Rogers was known for these lyrics.
The underlying meaning applies to this very topic.
Know when to hold them
Know when to fold them
Good advice in the form of a song
Maybe we should all sing along.

Somewhere a Rainbow is Weeping

Strange times are on the horizon
Darkness lurks all over our nation.
Praying for light and truth to be exposed
Brought out into the open and disposed.
Only a miracle can change hearts.
That is the only way healing starts.
Out of the shadows into the light
Hardened hearts come into sight.
Repentance and restoration of the soul
Is the only answer that will make things whole.
Rainbows are a combination of seven colors.
Rays of light reflecting and refracting through drops of rain.
A phenomenon in nature to help wash away our pain.
The flood narrative in the book of Genesis tells the story
When God looks at sin on earth and takes an inventory.

Then sends a flood to wash away humanity's corruption
Knowing it will create a direct interruption and intervention.
Afterwards God forms a rainbow in the sky as a sign of his
    promise
Never again to destroy the earth and bring destruction down
    upon us.
Somewhere a rainbow is weeping because God may be
questioning his pledge.
Kindness and peace between us need to return to erase the wedge.
We must close the divide and heal broken hearts by loving one
    another.
It's up to us now with help from God and our willingness to
    discover
A way to start again with renewed purpose and earn a chance
    for redemption.
So rainbows will no longer weep but shine with colorful rays
    of God's reflection.

Forever a Mother

Once you become a mother
A love blossoms inside unlike any other
From the very first time a mother hears her baby's heartbeat
Her own heart swells with joy and nothing has ever felt so
 sweet.
Once a mother, a protective nature arrives and never
 disappears.
It grows and changes facing many challenges throughout the
 years.
Even when a mother's child grows into a young adult
Her nurturing love continues to be the overpowering result.
And eventually when that child starts a family of his or her
 own
That caring, concerning nature/nurture continues to be shown.
Faced with many heartaches during this unusual and crazy
 year
The plight of future generations causes mothers to feel some
 fear.
Grandchildren bring an added dimension to a mother's life.
Her heart overflows with joy as this new facet takes flight.
Always innocent and precious they become the focus of her
 prayers
That life will be kind and forgiving and the bond will never
 fade away
Hoping to serve eternally as their ever-present guardian angel
In concert with God as a shield of protection from all and any
 danger.

Choices and Dilemmas

We make choices and face dilemmas every day
Making life exciting and dynamic in so many ways.
You should never be bored or unhappy when there's so much
    to do
Sports, dancing, crafts, reading and entertainment to name a
    few.
Sometimes you have to make a choice between two or more
    things.
Your time has to be divided into segments before the day
    begins.
Who knew retirement would keep you so busy?
Having too many options can make you feel dizzy.
You can become overwhelmed if you don't take control.
The people in your life you care about should take a large role.
Pursue righteousness, godliness, faith, love, patience and
    gentleness
Words spoken in the teachings of Jesus to ward off loneliness.
True happiness exists when you develop an inner joy and
    peace.
Time spent in prayer ensures that judicious choices do
    increase.
Give thanks to God for your blessings each day when you
    awake
Be wise, you have one life to live, there are no retakes to make.

The Door

Garage doors, front doors, screen doors, and sliding glass
    doors—
These are doors you encounter every day and probably many
    more.
Not a day goes by when you don't walk through a door
That opens up to outside adventures for you to explore.

Sometimes a friend's door will open and you're invited in.
It's your decision to enter; that's how it has always been.
Another more elusive door is one that opens to your heart;
When you let someone through they become a special part.

Hearts are like golden apples waiting to be caught.
Your heart's entrance leads to a gift that can never be bought.
A pledge of love becomes the gateway to this newfound world;
A fresh perspective unleashes as an optimistic dynamic is
    unfurled.

Later in time the door to heaven will open and invite you to
    enter.
If you believe, entrance is gained into God's eternal splendor.
This is the last door, the final door, the eternal door
To your soul's resting place that exists forevermore.

You Lift Me Up

My thoughts are often crushed and replaced
By crashing waves of doubt until they are erased.
Please lift me up when I am falling—
Hold me tight to prevent dislodging.
Keep me from drowning in my fears—
Send hope to wash away my tears.
It's hard to explain how I sometimes feel—
Regrets and insecurities seem so real.
Every time I turn around and take a step
Sadness unfolds and I wait for joy to intercept.
One step forward, two steps back—
How did I get so far off track?
Then I realize it's not within my power
So there's no need for me to cower.
He lifts me up and gives me strength
To face the day and restore my faith.
My enemy retreats when I call on You
Because God is on my side, He pulls me through.
The darkness subsides and I'm no longer afraid—
Your life-giving light and promise is displayed.

Unusual Friends

Afternoons with Copper Top

Copper Top is a bird.
He tweets but says no words.
He's majestic and serene
Flaps his wings when he wants to be seen.
His bright golden head is what you see
As he sits on top of our backyard tree.
Every day at 5:00 pm he appears
To join us not showing any fear
While we sip a glass of wine on our lanai.
Like clockwork he will come and fly by
Then sit on top of that lovely tree
Showing we are both created to be free
To appreciate the simple things in life
Connect spiritually on earth without strife.

Then one afternoon Copper Top did not appear.
Thinking the worst we felt some fear.
Instead a little yellow bird arrived
Made a little chirp so we could see
And landed gently on that same tree.
Sitting softly like a small fragile dove
Perhaps a sign from up above.
Little Copper Top came to relay
That the circle of life was on display.
Like Big Copper Top, he too came to say
Life goes on, nothing ever stays the same
You only get one chance to play the game
Enjoy every day as if it was your last
It's inevitable that it will soon be in the past.

The Pelican Parade

A spectacular parade of snowy white pelicans
Can be seen every day on our backyard lake.
Paddling quietly and gliding softly across the water
You can barely hear any sounds that they make.
Their long necks give their heads a unique long shape.
Their massive bills almost look like they could be fake.
A yellow plate forms on their upper bills
As they glide along so majestically still.
They have broad wings, thick bodies, short legs and square tails.
Every day we are fortunate to observe these magnificent details.
They come to visit around this time every year
A glorious sight when they all suddenly reappear.
During breeding season adult pelicans
Grow an unusual projection or horn
With yellow-orange bills and legs that adorn.
Black flight feathers are visible when their wings are spread.
Dipping their beaks into water to catch fish
They hardly ever have to lift up their heads.
Although among the heaviest flying birds in the world
They are superb soarers as their wings are unfurled.
Oh, to appreciate the beauty right before our eyes.
God's showcase unfolds and becomes a wonderful surprise.
Why not "unplug?"
Take in the sights and sounds of your surroundings
To fully comprehend what God has created.
It is truly magnificent and absolutely astounding.
Smell the fresh air
Disconnect from the news and your phone
The simplicity, the pace and patience of nature is shown
Like the slow, methodical and luxurious pelican parade
God's marvelous world outside your door is displayed.

The Puppy Who Wore a Red Tutu

In The Villages, dogs are treated like kings and queens.
They are cared for like babies, their owners will never be
    mean.
They ride in strollers, take naps and eat treats all day long
Pampered and petted constantly, nothing ever goes wrong.
Anthropomorphism is the phenomenon of treating pets like
    humans.
Out and about one day, I thought it must have been an
    illusion.
When I saw a puppy riding in a stroller dressed in a frilly red
    tutu
To top it off they picked her up like a newborn calling her Fou
    Fou.
Next thing you know there will be treatments for Doggie
    A.D.D.
Prescription medicine for anxiety and doggie psychologists
    too.

Squish

On a warm afternoon, a bird flew into our garage.
He came all by himself without an entourage.
Scared and frightened, he didn't know how to fly out.
He just squealed a little and kept flailing all about.

He settled on the top of the garage door opening.
We were afraid it might squish him or break his wing.
To lighten the situation we called him Squish by name.
Our new feathered friend and buddy, he quickly became.

Then Squish finally did fly out with a fluttering zoom.
Another bird was waiting for him or so we assumed.
The second bird, to Squish, seemed to say,
"Glad you're okay" and to us, "have a good day!"

Now each night while sitting out on our lanai
Squish stops by often and tips his wing just to say hi.
He perches on a nearby tree and sings us a song.
I'm sure he's saying thank you but I could be wrong.

There's a lesson to be learned from this story.
We are blessed when we give God all the glory.
Life's little surprises come in all shapes and sizes.
God keeps us alert with nature's sweet surprises.

Puffy and the Taffy Pull

Puffy was a fluffy white rabbit
Who had a very unusual habit.
He loved Bonomo's Turkish taffy.
You may think this is all too daffy
It really is true and I have a friend as a witness
Who can prove this is not just childhood silliness.
Puffy only liked taffy that had a vanilla flavor
Chocolate or strawberry was not in his favor.
I would give him a little piece
Then he would pull it up with his 2 front teeth
Into long white taffy strands
Using his buck teeth because he had no hands.
Every day Puffy enjoyed an old-fashioned taffy pull
Until he got tired or felt too full
I was always afraid he might end up with a tooth ache
Which then would turn into a big mistake.
Do they have dentists for bunnies
Or only in the comic strip funnies?
Puffy was my favorite childhood pet for many years
When I think of him I chuckle then cry some crocodile tears.

We Called the Cat Mariah

I was never lucky enough to own a dog
Only hamsters, fish, turtles and a frog.
Once I brought home an adorable stray kitten
My mother wasn't so pleased or as smitten.
We called the cat Mariah
Although I preferred Papaya.
She was cute but incredibly wild
Overly active like a mischievous child.

I later had a cat named Black Beard
The name now seems so weird
Even though we thought it was a boy
Until "she" had several bundles of joy.
Five or six little kittens were born
Causing us at the time to be forlorn
Until they stole away our hearts
We hated to ever have to part.

Many different cats came in and out of my life
Way too many as I refused to listen to any advice.
Mickey and Minnie, YoYo and Ralph to name a few
I think I even had one called Pepe Le Pew.
They were mischievous at times, a part of their charm
They would lay across my keyboard meaning no harm
Because they were playful, independent and curious
Joyful companions rendering my home especially glorious.

Barbara Welsh

Black Cats and Superstitions

It must be hard to be a black cat
Because black cats get a bad rap.
They're often associated with witches
And other scary things that hide in ditches.

If a black cat crosses your path, misfortune follows
This is one of many superstitions hard to swallow.
They may cause you to scream in fright
When they go bump in the middle of the night.

It is often said 13 is an unlucky number
Or opening an umbrella inside is a bummer.
You should never walk underneath an open ladder
Because later on it could negatively matter.

As a kid, stepping on a crack in the sidewalk
Meant you'll break your mother's back.
Superstitions are present everywhere you go
Many people feel the impact and will say so.

What if we do a reversal
To initiate a good-luck rehearsal
Then black cats would be welcome in every home
Delivering good fortune so witches would be left to roam.

Words and the Personal Touch

Yada Yada Yada

When someone says yada, yada, yada what comes to mind?
Do you get offended and think they're being unkind?
Do you try to guess what words they meant to include
Or just let it go thinking they are totally rude?
Do you think yada, yada, yada has replaced blah, blah, blah?
Does it mean anything different or just more of the same hoopla?
Where in the world did yada, yada, yada originate anyway?
Actually it was first heard across your television airwaves
On the 153rd episode of the American sitcom "Seinfeld."
You probably laughed so hard that your face turned red.
If you remember when George's new girlfriend
Said yada, yada, yada at the end of a personal story
Driving him crazy and causing him to worry.
Today when a sentence is too lengthy to recite in full
Yada, yada, yada is often used to cut out some of the bull.
It also may eliminate a disparaging response
That is predictable, repetitive or tedious
By not becoming too demeaning, dicey or devious.
So have some fun and whatever you do...
Smile, laugh, tell a joke and Yada Yada Yada!

ISH

Ish is a suffix that recently became an independent word.
A new adjective formed from a noun is now very often heard.
Ish can mean "unaccountable" or "to some extent."
Meaning "to some degree" or "an estimate of time" is ish's
    intent.
Acting childish or saying you hope to arrive 10ish or shortly
    after.
Never having to be accurate and precise from now and
    hereafter.
When asked your age you can say 50ish or 60ish so you avoid
    the truth.
Isn't *ish* the best suffix and word ever? It's a chance to act like
    a sleuth.
Is *ish* in the dictionary and is it acceptable as a word in
    Scrabble?
Yes, *ish* is a word meaning approximately, a little like to
    dabble.
Ish became a valid and accepted Scrabble word on February 4,
    2020.
It seems that these new funny words, like *ish* and iffy, are said
    quite aplenty.
BTW, did you know when texting, *"ish"* means "insert sarcasm
    here"?
Never heard of that one at least not so far this year.
So are you kind of bookish, freakish, babyish, skittish, or
    boorish?
Or from another country so are you British, Danish, English or
    Spanish?

A Comfort Zone Clone

Take a step out of your comfort zone
Start on a different course into the unknown
Stop procrastinating and take a chance
How else will you ever advance?
Stop the excuses and ramp up your focus
It's nothing that requires any hocus pocus.
You're never too old to try something new
Make a new bucket list that's what you can do.
You live in a world of infinite possibilities
Have faith in your own innate capabilities.
You don't have to sky dive or jump off a cliff
God will not let you go that far adrift.
Life is too short to keep finding ways to postpone
Do you want to turn into a comfort zone clone?

Veritas

Truth is mighty and will prevail
It does not change by any scale.
Veritas is a latin phrase meaning to analyze and see
That the truth can really set you free.
The opposite of veritas is vice
A defect in which you may pay a price.
Veritas is a virtue or ideal
Proving that honesty leads to what is real.
A lie will eventually be exposed
At some point its validity will be disclosed.
When something false is repeated over and over
It becomes more believable with each exposure
Until no one can tell what is fact or what is not
Until the perpetrator of the lie is caught.
Absolute truth is transcendent and never changes
Like God's approachable words on the Bible's pages.
They remain the same yesterday, today and tomorrow
The more you read, study and decide to follow.

#Hashtags

Hash is a food with a mixture of ingredients to eat.
Hash brown potatoes can be a tasty breakfast treat.
Hash also is a form of cannabis you shouldn't ever meet.
Tag is a game of chasing and catching another player
Or a way to mark something as a type of conveyor.
So what is a hashtag you see used on social networks
    everywhere?
#Hashtag here, #hashtag there, how many hashtags do I have
    to bear?
Hashtags do make it easier to find messages with a certain
    content or theme
A way to connect to a specific topic, event or anything in
    between.
But is there a hashtag able to change your age or weight
Or one that miraculously substitutes love for hate?
Is there a hashtag that erases the division and anger seen today
Or that can bring unity, peace and hope that lasts forever and
    will stay?
Many hashtags are nonexistent today and to some might seem
    odd.
They are #Faith, #Trust, #Belief and most important of all is
    ###God!

Oodles of Doodles

Doodles are often considered windows to the soul
They may uncover traits you may not even know.
Doodles are not silly but evidence of a sharp mind
Helping to maintain focus and not get behind.
Hand scribbling random things on a piece of paper
Serves as a distraction or a method of escape.
Doodles allow personality types to be revealed
There are all types of things doodles can yield.
If you draw circles you are loving and honest.
Doodles of flowers indicate you are gentle and modest.
A tidy drawing is an indication of a happy home life.
A messy doodle means your life could have strife.
Doodles of squares may mean you want to be in control.
Arrows pointing up means your life is on a roll.
So here are some questions to ponder about doodles
Picture oodles of doodles and no cheating with Google.
If you doodle a noodle

Barbara Welsh

Will you turn into a poodle?
If you doodle a duck
Are you out of luck
Will you turn into a truck?
If you doodle a wombat
Will you get big and fat?
Doodling all your lost socks
Might turn you into a falling rock.
Will doodles of butterflies
Give you a bad case of hives?
So what makes us scribble, doodle or make a little sketch?
Is it to keep us from going crazy; feeling like you're on the edge
Wanting to give up and jump off a ledge
No, we all like making oodles of doodles
There's no need to ask anyone for approval.
So that's the whole kit and caboodle.

Seeing Through a Different Lens

Seeing Through a Different Lens

Prayer and meditation can shape your thinking
Like reading a self-help book from a recent printing
To keep your mind anchored and in focus
Erasing false prophecies and any hocus pocus.
Prayer turns worry and fear into faith and hope
When you trust that God will work all things out
Making it much easier for you to cope.
It can redirect and change your perspective
So that you will think and be more objective.
If you pray about a problem and have faith
A solution will be found in most every case.
Praying empowers you with peace of mind
To avoid living day to day as if you were blind.
It can help you to see the bigger picture
Like a high-tech camera with a clear exposure.
When you look at life through a different lens
It gives your psyche a needed cleanse.
Seeing things through someone else's eyes
Clears the way for you to become empathetic and wise.
It's a time in your life filled with surprises and a new
    revelation
Your vision has sharpened and entered a period of
    reconciliation.

Each and Every Memory

In your mind's eye each and every memory may be sweet
Remembering the times when your life was complete.
Then some others you may look back on as being bad
When times were not so happy and you were sad.
A compilation of every memory makes up the past
Like a diary we carry around hoping the recollection will last.
Memories both good and bad allow us to learn and grow
Teaching important life lessons sometimes fast, sometimes slow.
Memories are the glue that binds pieces of our life together
Consoling our spirits like a warm blanket or sweater.
Memories may fade as the years go by and depart
Invisible to the eye but still felt by the heart.
Moments today become memories tomorrow.
Hold onto those that reflect times of joy, not sorrow
The heart that truly loves never forgets
A proverb to live by that you'll never regret.
Don't cry because yesterday is now just a memory
Smile because it happened...
It's now part of your own documentary.

Keeping Hope Alive

When you lose someone that you have always leaned on
You hold back tears looking forward to a new day's dawn.
Your heart may break but you're still alive
Lost in many ways but maintaining hope in order to survive.
How can you replace constructive analysis that is hard to find?
A perspective that opened your eyes when many are so blind.
Can we keep hope alive while the truth is often hidden
When honesty is disguised and free speech is forbidden?
Hope can emerge even in our mourning and sorrow
If not today or right away then definitely tomorrow.
Your heart still beats and you're still breathing
Trying to understand what is God's real meaning.
By helping another person and showing love and
    understanding
It takes the focus off yourself to discover what God is
    commanding.
Seizing what you have learned by keeping hope alive
Expectations for a radiant new future in which to strive.
Even though you miss that positive voice that was often
    misunderstood
In reality we learn that God's plan will always lead to all that
    is good.

The Person in the Mirror

If you lack confidence and are feeling low
Look in the mirror to see what your reflections show.
Mirrors reveal what we look like not who we are
Sparkling on the outside like a celestial star.
Don't be crippled by your own self doubt
Believe in yourself and your confidence will shine out.
The person in the mirror is often your harshest critic
Don't be so hard on yourself, be proud, not so psychoanalytic.
The person in the mirror determines their own happiness.
Stay in control, don't blame someone else when experiencing
sadness.
Life is like a mirror, it may not always be what you hoped it
would be
It is a gage of what we allow others to see.
An image of dissatisfaction may show up once in awhile
Then the next day it may turn back into a beautiful smile.
The way you reflect the world around you
Is the direct expression of the world within you.
In the mirror, we see a reflection of our outside appearance
But in our heart we discover our soul's emittance.
Proverbs 27:19 says that a mirror's image is only one part
"As water reflects the face, so one's life reflects the heart."

Winning the Battle in Your Mind

Many of life's battles are won or lost in the mind.
Negative thoughts may lead to actions that are often unkind.
Out-of-control thinking will cause fear and frustration
Leading to feelings of defeat and low expectations.
There's a constant tug-of-war between good and bad.
The winner will determine if you are mostly happy or sad.
Your life moves in the direction of your strongest thoughts
Fighting toxic beliefs to avoid getting overwhelmed and
    distraught.
Fix your mind on what is honorable, right and pure
Then a positive state of mind will become natural for sure.
Win the insecurity battle and discover that you are worthy
By changing your thinking you can eliminate the worry.
Remove the lies that you hear and replace them with truth.
Lean closer to God and you'll soon have the proof
That you're winning the battle raging in your mind
To achieve peace and harmony that is not easy to find.

Life's Game of Chutes and Ladders

While visiting my grandchildren we played several games -
One in particular should be in the Board Games Hall of Fame.
Chutes and Ladders is a classic game introduced in 1943.
It was fun to play and our favorite game we all did agree.
If a player lands on a good deed they can shimmy up a ladder
Or sometimes they're sent down a chute like a mad hatter.
It teaches young kids numbers up to 100 and basic game plays
Like taking turns, dealing with bad luck, and how strategy
    pays.
Chutes and Ladders teaches how much of our successes in life
Come from previous mistakes, failures and sometimes strife.
Children learn that they can't win every time
To have patience and allow others a chance to shine.
It is special to watch grandchildren grow right before our eyes.
They are special gifts from God, full of life and really very
    wise.
They teach us that life is simple, sweet and filled with
    adventure
Giving and receiving love unconditionally without fear of
    surrender
Speaking openly and honestly without hesitation
Not worried about what others think or their evaluation.
If we accept one another without judgment like little children
    do
Ladders that lead to a light of serenity will forever shine
    through.

Places of Safety

Finding Your Place of Safety

Have we gotten so far from the truth
That we have lost the safety net of our youth?
Has the unthinkable become the unquestionable
Having to accept many things we find objectionable?
Something is missing when you believe that you alone
Occupy the center of the universe.
When God is the focal point, your life is the reverse
It's a place where love, peace and harmony exist
And hate, resentment and bitterness are quickly dismissed.
When you are content in every situation you face
You can focus on what matters so regrets and lies are erased.
When God is the center you develop a shield of protection
A secure place of safety with an all-powerful connection.

A Million Raindrops

If a million raindrops fall from a bright blue sky
Will they wash all heartaches and cares away?
Can the rhythm of the wind calm your mind,
Chasing burdens away to be left behind?
A rainbow is sometimes seen after a rainstorm
When the sun breaks through clouds that form.
It evokes feelings of serenity and peace
Allowing solidarity and thankfulness to be released.
As white light shines through water droplets
An array of colors is displayed like pretty composites.
In Genesis, a rainbow appears after a worldwide flood
To remove sinful and evil-minded people to be judged.
These are not just words on a page
It gives a glimpse of God's mighty rage.
So when millions of raindrops fall from a sky that is blue
Is it a sign that if we change our ways and become honest and
     true,
God's love and shield of protection will continue to shine
     through?

Heart Lines

Whenever You are near
You take away the fear
You are a bright light in a dark sky
Your radiance is the reason why.

Just as we feel warmth when the sun shines
We also sense the rhythm of our heart lines
Let them vibrate and glow so bright
That they will reflect God's holy light.

We are created in the image of God
So our lives never need a façade
Like birds floating upon the sea
All heart lines are meant to be.

We're caught up in Your powerful spell
Hearing a voice that sounds like a crystal bell
Similar to rays of light on a dark, rainy day
A fervent yearning for peace remains in play.

Anxious Thoughts

Anxious thoughts come from the heart
Restlessness leads to a need to restart.
Your feelings seem to tumble all around
Like ping pong balls bouncing to the ground.
Overcrowded schedules with no downtime to be found
Insufficient rest and busyness breeds negative thoughts
Time to reassess, slow down and change your course.
Take some time each day to say a prayer
Give someone a compliment to show you care.
Live, love, and enjoy the beauty of each new dawn
Fill each day with gladness before the curtains are drawn.
Fight worries, anxiety and fears
Lean on God to eradicate your tears
Never lose an opportunity to search for God's peace
Then anxious thoughts will fade away and not increase.

Noises

Block out the noises of life that make you mad
Those of envy, hate, and actions you consider bad.
Avoid negative people who bring you down
Sounds of gossip and complaining that surround
Like thunder when it roars during stormy weather.
Longing for a calming breeze soft enough to lift a feather.
Listen to the musical rhythm of a harmonic symphony
Reminding us of God's voice bringing forth a fresh epiphany.
A friend or lover's tender words comfort you like a gentle rain.
These noises promote a life free of anger and emotional pain.
A difference arises when you receive and perceive a sound
Sending a signal that prepares and tells you how to respond.
Filter out and remove noises that you wish not to hear
Your life will become uncluttered, fresh, and crystal clear.

Worthy Alliances

Who you spend time with can have an effect
Only you can decide to accept or reject
What people say and how they act.
Hold your head high, don't overreact.

True friends uplift you helping you to feel worthwhile
With a compliment, a word of encouragement or a smile
Others make you feel inferior
Bragging and acting so superior.

You feel meritless, unimportant and sad
Like you never do the right thing, always feeling bad.
Then God will gently whisper how special you are
 Deserving of love, the real truth comes from afar.

He created you to be precisely who you are; wonderfully
made.
Criticism has no effect when knowledge of His presence is
displayed.
Don't let public opinion determine what is right or wrong
The pursuit of truth and honesty will make you strong.

Form relationships around honorable things
Let alliances be centered on what faithfulness brings.
Powerful forces will come into play
If you allow God to lead the way.

Inner Peace

If you hold on to happy thoughts
And let go of those that are naught
Then inner peace can begin to be a part
Of a smile that radiates from your heart.

Try to accept all things that have occurred
Knowing you can't alter them or the world.
But you can change yourself by making improvements
One step at a time initiating desirable achievements.

Maintain harmonious relationships with friends.
Stay away from negative people who condescend.
You can then remain faithful to your highest ideals
And not be affected by things that take away the zeal.

If you long for anxiety to cease
And you want to achieve inner peace:
First forgive yourself and others
Then picture life as a tapestry of brilliant colors.

Don't be bound by the world's demands
Ask God for guidance because He understands.
Never covet anyone else's riches or talents
Trust that you can cultivate a grateful balance.

Being in the Spotlight

Some people need to be in the spotlight
Enjoying the splendor of the limelight
Always the center of public attention.
The person that everyone mentions
Talks about, interviews and photographs
Fans asking them for their autograph.
Loving the glitz, fireworks, and applause.
Is this realistic or should we stop to pause
And acknowledge the illumination within us
That helps to distinguish what is true and just.
When we only exist to be in a temporal spotlight
Loneliness may intervene on any given day or night.
Do we deserve all the praise and merit
Or should God receive the glory and credit?
Spotlights ought to highlight our internal faith
Shining out radiating His amazing love and grace.

Healing a Broken Heart

Love is a lesson that isn't taught in school
You don't learn it from a book as a general rule.
Hearts are broken when you lose someone
As the score in the game of life is lost or won.
Whether it's your choice or not to say goodbye
You try to hide your tears when you want to cry.
How do you hide a broken heart
Do you hear a sound when it breaks apart?
You can chase a new dream when it's right for you
By focusing on what's positive to shine a light on what to do.
If you call or visit a friend who has a more pressing need
It takes your mind off yourself saying it's time to proceed.
God provides a road map when you seek direction on your
    path
By loving, living and letting go of bitterness and wrath.
The tiniest bit of hope that dwells in a heart that is broken
Will mend with kind words spoken and thoughts unspoken.

All the Best Things

The Most Meaningful Gift

Some people are excellent gift givers
They always choose something that really delivers.
Others have trouble knowing what to buy
They purchase something then wonder why.

A meaningful gift creates an impact
Whether it is big in size or compact.
This gift eventually becomes a treasured item
Something needed, wanted and especially vital.

This type of gift is meant to last
Its value will never be surpassed.
The longer retained the more it is cherished
It endures forever; never needs to be embellished.

This special gift may even change someone's life
Like a blessing, always intended to cause delight
Imparting a smile to the receiver's face
Beyond description and hard to erase.

The most meaningful gift is incredibly generous
Wrapped in love and decorated with tenderness.
It is when someone gives away their heart
Along with a promise to never depart.

Acts of Kindness

More than a friend you are to me
Giving strength that only I can see
Blessing my life more than you'll ever know
A deeper love that becomes hard to show
Kindness and concern is so often revealed
Like a shadow serving as a protective shield
Little things you may say or do
Never wavering, always true
When I see your bright smile
My cares evaporate for awhile
A giving nature and humble heart
Reveals a warmth that only you impart.

The Magic Suitcase

Grandma has a magic suitcase
Recently grounded, not able to go any place.
Grandma and her suitcase have been home for awhile
Not available to visit and make her little ones smile.
Grandchildren were missed when they had to stay home.
Grandparents couldn't travel feeling isolated and alone.
The Magic Suitcase will soon be back in service
Ready and willing to fulfill its purpose.
It is filled with little treasures that cause delight
Nothing dangerous or scary that can cause a fright.
After the Magic Suitcase arrives gifts begin to appear
In front of bedroom doors or somewhere near.
Every morning each grandchild will take a look
To find little trinkets, toys, games or a book.
It is a surprise and mini miracle every day
Until grandma and her magic suitcase go away.
Seeing the eyes of excitement is a special treat
To make Grandma's visit and life complete.

Joyful Raindrops

Can you move clouds across the sky
To produce rain and thunder if you try?
Only God can do these things
With the endless love that He brings.

Raindrops can wash away the pain
Leaving remnants of hope for you to gain.
Teardrops that fall today like raindrops from your eyes
Tomorrow will glisten transforming into a bright sunrise.

In your darkest hour
You can feel the power.
The troubles and trials you may face
Joyful raindrops will erase.

Faith is like the sun shining through the haze
It is more alleviating than a lover's gaze.
Faith lifts you up when you fall
Will never cause you to falter or stall.

When faithfulness stretches to the sky
The heart does not doubt or wonder why
Joyful raindrops form from God's celestial love
Resembling alluring stars seen from high above.

Faith of a Tiny Seed

Faith begins as a tiny seed
With a whisper made to take heed.
When the seed is planted in fertile soil
It will flourish and begin to uncoil
Growing roots reaching out to form an anchor
Increasing trust to help find a longed-for answer.
Today, our perspective is often shaped by social media
Losing touch with reality and yearning for things remedial.
A simple act of kindness or a faith-filled prayer
Takes a backseat to materialism so we are unaware
That these things do not make your life complete
Eventually you start to feel empty and incomplete.
Faith can have a mountain-moving impact
By believing all things are possible, the seed unwraps
And in time it becomes an exquisite flower
When faith of a tiny seed coincides with God's invincible
    power.

Writing a Poem

Writing a poem is like creating a sculpture
You have to start with a solid infrastructure.
First select a theme, topic or life emotion
That is relatable and worthy of your devotion.
Brainstorm and write down some words and phrases
Until you initiate a flow that ultimately will unveil praises.
Then consider words that blend together and usually rhyme.
This process takes thought and an unspecified amount of time
To whittle it down to create a picturesque work of art
That will captivate the reader from the very start.
Relinquish it to God and He will tell you what to write
Soon the verses come alive into the effulgent world's light.

Matzo Ball Soup

Matzo Ball soup served in a bowl
Is a natural elixir for a tender soul.
When you are feeling sad and a little down
Soup is the best comfort food to be found.
It lifts your spirits when made with love from the heart
To lighten your mood with the warmth it imparts.
The first little sip can make you feel more alive
Especially when you've had a bad day it tends to revive.
Sometimes it is called the "Jewish penicillin"
Because it provides a jolt of healthy nutrition.
It's a symbol of faith and friendship to me
Like a balm or tonic it becomes clearer to see
That brighter days are on the horizon tomorrow
With close friends around to alleviate the sorrow.

Christmas Snow Globes and Sparkle / Poem on Page 61

Acknowledgments

Debbie Campana
My personal editor who has read, critiqued and edited every poem in this book. Without her none of these poems would have come to fruition

Phyllis Schechtman
My administrative assistant who organized my first 100 poems and has read each one written since and given her approval.

My Three Children: Jennifer Caldwell, Stephen Caldwell, and Andrew Caldwell; their spouses: Peter Farah, Liberty Caldwell and Stephanie Caldwell; and seven grandchildren: Nyah, Layla, Kira, Finley, Evelyn, Hudson, and Quinn who are the loves of my life.

My Support Team: Debbie, Phyllis, Bonnie, Pat, Patti, Valerie, Carol, Jean, Judy

The Terrific Team of Ten
They began as a simple lunchtime trend.
They are talented, thoughtful teammates
Who tactfully teach each other how to be true.
They seem tacky because they wear tutus
Tease, text, and make treats so not to be blue.
They remain tolerant, tactful and transforming
Their commitment to each other keeps them in line
Sharing a tremendous tendency to treasure
True friendship during these trying times.

The Message of Dance / Poem on Page 31

About the Author

 Barbara C. Welsh is a poet, editor, and retired teacher—among many other accomplishments. She started writing poetry during the COVID-19 pandemic. While learning a new dance online she wrote her first poem, "Hoping, Praying, and Dancing."

Since then she has written over 230 poems, many of which have been published in *The Villages Daily Sun, Poet's Corner,* and in the *Village Neighbors* magazine.

Barbara loves to dance, especially line dancing, Zumba and, more recently, cardio drumming. She was in the Gemstone Dancers, a performing dance group, and is a volunteer counselor at the Pregnancy and Family Care Center in Leesburg, FL.

A member of The Florida Authors and Publishers Association (FAPA), Florida Writers Association (FWA), the Writers League of The Villages (WLOV), and Associate Member of the Academy of American Poets, Barbara has a Bachelor of Science degree in Home Economics and Education from West Virginia Wesleyan College and a Master of Arts degree in Family Studies from Montclair State University in N.J.

Barbara lives in The Villages, Florida with her husband, Michael Yankus. She has three children, four stepchildren, and seventeen grandchildren.

Contact her at Barbaratwoten@gmail.com.

The Pelican Parade / Poem on Page 100

About the Illustrator

Manhattan-born award-winning illustrator Donna Yankus grew up in a carnival setting and was an honor student at the School of Visual Arts in New York City, earning a degree in Fine Arts, Illustration/Cartooning, and later on, Art History. She is also a special needs teacher. She currently volunteers for local non-for-profit organizations, including the Islip Arts Council, is Firefighter/Fire Police/ Fire Chaplain at her local fire department in Islip Terrace. Her passions include volunteer hours at the New York Marine Rescue center, in the Long Island Aquarium, where she is not only working to protect the local marine life and environment of Long Island, but also providing beautiful pieces of art for various fundraising events.

Donna has worked with Disney, Jim Henson, Hallmark, and Reuters. She has also designed and illustrated multiple murals for countless amusement park rides.

Her other passions include surfing, running, playing the ukulele, video game design, and going on adventures with her family.

Donna lives in Islip Terrace, New York, with her husband and two sons.

Contact her at https://dyankusdesign.godaddysites.com

Keeping Hope Alive / Poem on Page 117

Made in the USA
Columbia, SC
31 October 2022

70196341R00080